CO$_2$
Temperature
and Humidity

CO$_2$
Temperature
and Humidity

by D. Gold
edited by Ed Rosenthal

Quick American Archives

ISBN# 0-932551-24-6

A previous edition, CO_2, *Temperature, Humidity, Ventilation and Odor Control*, was published by D. Gold.

Book Design: Ed Rosenthal
Cover Design: Jane Klein
Cover Drawing: Pauline Phung
Illustrations: Jim Todd
Typography: BookPrep

Published by: Quick American Archives
              P.O. Box 429477
              San Francisco, CA 94142-9477

Table of Contents

Introduction

CO_2 - The Invisible Ally

30% to 40% Increase in Growth Rate

Of all the high-tech growth increasing methods available to the hobbyist or larger producer, the addition of CO_2 is probably the quickest, simplest, and most reliable single procedure that can be used.

A growth rate increase of 30% to 40% is typical of grow areas with elevated levels of CO_2.

Why CO_2 Helps

Photosynthesis is the process in which plants "inhale" CO_2 from the air and combine it with water, using light energy to produce sugar and oxygen.

An adequate supply of CO_2 is necessary for plants to photosynthesize. A plant will quickly use up the CO_2 immediately surrounding it. Since a plant cannot move around in search of fresh air, if nothing is done to move the air, the plant will suffer from CO_2 depletion and will stop producing sugars needed for energy and growth. If the air is moved, by a fan or other means of ventilation, the plant has far more CO_2 available to it, and will grow more vigorously. If, in addition to moving the air, CO_2 is added in large quantities, the plant will respond with an enormous increase in the growth rate.

Chapter 1

CO_2 Depletion

Many hobbyists fail to realize the importance of CO_2.

In a closed area growing plants rapidly use up the CO_2 in the environment and replace it with oxygen. When the plants use up about one third of the CO_2, which doesn't take very long if the plants are large or in rapid growth phase, plant growth virtually stops.

The situation becomes most serious in areas without any internal air circulation, such as a fan. This is because a microclimate forms around the leaves. The small area directly around the leaves rapidly depletes of CO_2. Even though there may be adequate CO_2 levels a few inches from the plants, the leaves themselves are not in direct contact with air containing enough CO_2.

CO_2 replacement is necessary even in a room with good internal circulation. A closed room full of healthy growing plants can use up the CO_2 in less than an hour. A large room with small cuttings or seedlings doesn't use up the CO_2 nearly as quickly but the CO_2 still must be replaced.

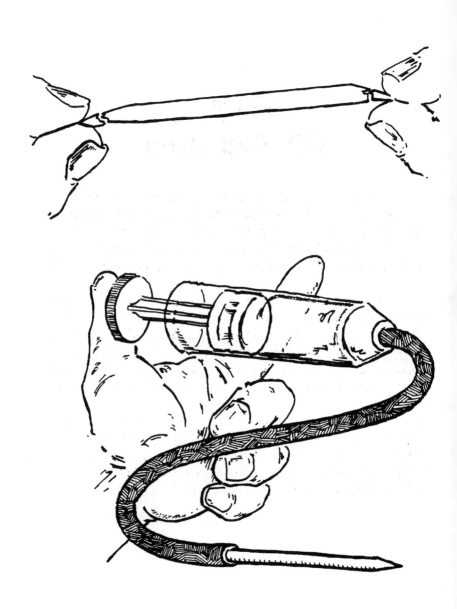

Chapter 2

Measuring Airborne CO_2

CO_2 is calculated and measured in **parts per million - ppm.** Country air contains about 300 ppm. City air usually contains about 400 ppm. Most researchers put the ideal level for maximum growth rate at about 1500 ppm, or five times the amount of CO_2 found in fresh air.

Inexpensive CO_2 Tester

The simple inexpensive test kit pictured here is available from a number of garden supply distributors across the country. Each glass tube is good for just one test, and costs about $7.50. This is a small price to pay for the benefits that come from proper CO_2 enhancement, no matter what size the garden.

Using the CO_2 Test Kit

1. Place the short piece of flexible plastic tubing on the end of the plastic syringe.

2. Carefully snap off each end of the glass tube.

3. Push the plunger on the syringe all the way in to clear any air.

4. Draw back the plunger to the 100 cc mark in the air to be tested.

5. Place the glass tube in the open end of the flexible tubing.

6. Push firmly on the plastic plunger and slowly force the air through the glass tube. The entire process should take about one minute.

7. Notice the white powder in the tube change color (either red or blue depending on the brand).

8. When all the air in the syringe has been forced through the glass tube, the CO_2 level is indicated by the top of the colored band in the indicator tube. (See drawing on page 2.)

Chapter 3

Before You Start

Before choosing a CO_2 production system for your growing pleasure, keep in mind that CO_2 is only one of several interdependent growth-enhancing factors. If any one of these factors is forgotten or ignored, all your efforts with CO_2 will be wasted. These factors are:

1. Ventilation
2. Temperature
3. Humidity

Chapter 4

Air Circulation and Ventilation

If CO_2 is injected into a room with no internal air circulation, it immediately falls to the floor and stays there, or it leaks out the cracks in the door and around the baseboard. Even with moderate air circulation, such as a small fan, CO_2 settles and does not reach the leaves.

Lots of Fans

The key to maintaining even CO_2 levels throughout the grow room lies in internal circulation. Quite simply, the most successful grow rooms have the most fans. Plants seem to benefit by a constant blast of CO_2 laden air. In addition to the fresh CO_2, the constant motion of the plant parts causes tiny tears in the tissue. These heal to form a much stronger stem system, which is important when it comes time to support the abundant and heavy fruit, vegetables, and flowers that result from high-tech growing.

Some growers use a double layer approach to air circulation. Powerful oscillating fans are placed above the canopy formed by the plants, and a second fan system is placed below the canopy, blowing over the lower stems, and the pots, slabs, cubes or other hydroponic medium or support system. (See drawing on page 6.)

Vertical Air Circulation

Blowing air vertically helps disperse CO_2 evenly and prevents flat spots (microclimates) in the growing chamber. It also helps prevent mold and mildew. The cool floor air is pumped out over the hot lights, lowering the overall temperature.

Ventilation and Air Exchange

Even when supplying CO_2 ventilation is necessary to remove airborne wastes created by the plants. These include hormones and other plant chemicals.

Basics of Ventilation

Assuming that CO_2 is supplemented, high speed periodic evacuation is desirable to accomplish the air exchange as quickly as possible. **If CO_2 is not supplemented, ventilate like crazy.**

Squirrel Cages

Although there are some makeshift applications that work fairly well, it is hard to beat a **squirrel cage** or **shaded pole** blower. The models in the 200 cfm (cubic feet per minute) range are relatively inexpensive and work in closet sized growing chambers.

The 465 cfm blower is probably the most popular one sold. It usually costs under $100 for a very safe and reliable exhaust system.

A pump with a capacity of about 980 cubic feet per minute will discharge the air equivalent in a 10ft. × 10ft. × 10ft. room in about one minute. However, the incoming air mixes with the outgoing air, so one minute of operation results in a 50% reduction of stale air. A three minute cycle would change the air almost completely.

The most efficient grow rooms utilize two fans - one to pump in fresh air and one to remove stale air. This method moves the air very quickly. Most experts agree that two 465 cfm blowers operated in this manner probably do the job better than a single 980.

One consideration that amateur growers often overlook when first installing the fan is the noise/vibration factor. Although the noise of the fan is quite low, it operates at a high rate of speed with quite a bit of centrifugal force. If anchored directly to the ceiling, the fan could set up a subtle vibration that shakes the entire house or apartment building for five minutes every hour, just like clockwork.

One of the ways to reduce the vibration is to mount the fan on a piece of plywood, and hang the wood from the ceiling on stout cords a few inches long. A flexible ductwork is constructed to pump the exhausted air into the ceiling.

Chapter 5

Monitoring Temperature and Humidity

Gardeners monitor heat and humidity levels by using thermometers to measure temperature and hygrometers to measure relative humidity. The desired ranges are:

1. Temperature: The best range is above 85 and below 95 degrees Fahrenheit with CO_2 injection. Some experiments indicate that maximum growth rate occurs at around 95 degrees with CO_2 at 1500 ppm. There are other experiments that indicate that CO_2 enhancement does not do much for the growth rate below 75 degrees. It is also recognized as a good practice to keep the temperature below 85 degrees if the ambient air is being used without CO_2 enhancement.

2. Humidity: In the literature, it is often stated that the grower should keep the relative humidity above 40% and below 65%.

The 65% point is OK as a rule of thumb, but problems can still occur in the high fifties and low sixties range. Most fungus stop growing when humidity levels are low and there is constant internal circulation from powerful oscillating fans.

Gardeners sometimes overlook the humidity build-up during the dark hours. Some growers have their fans set on the same timer as the lights. However this is the time when molds are most likely to grow. To prevent attack the fans should be left on during the dark hours to prevent mold.

Some gardeners use a small heater to keep the temperature up and the humidity down during the lights' off cycle. A de-humidifier serves both purposes, raising temperature and lowering humidity.

As the temperature drops, the relative humidity increases. Hot air can hold more water than cold air. The same amount of water dissolved in cold air creates a higher humidity than when dissolved in hot air. An automatic humidistat operating a blower or de-humidifier can be left on during the dark hours. The well-equipped growth chamber with remote hygrometers and thermometers allows the grower to observe the conditions in the grow room during the dark hours, without disrupting the dark cycle.

Chapter 6

Temperature Control

The heat output of multiple High-Intensity Discharge lights can create a considerable problem for the grower. It may be difficult to keep the heat below 80 degrees without CO_2, or below 95 degrees with CO_2, especially in the summer. Gardeners lucky enough to have a basement grow room will appreciate it during the heat of August.

There are many solutions to the heat problem. Some are simple but expensive to set up and operate, and others are inventive and inexpensive. Let's start at the top.

Air Conditioners

Installing an air conditioner is a quick and simple fix for many heat build-up problems. Simply put one in the window, set the vent on closed position so that the CO_2 laden air is recycled, and set the thermostat to turn the device on at 95 degrees. Most gardeners don't seem to mind the cost, considering the benefits. But those monthly electric bills can become real worriers.

Sensible Use of the Air Conditioner

There are some climates and conditions where an air conditioner is just about the only way possible to keep the temperature down to desired levels. Even so, there are a number of steps that can be taken to keep electrical use to a minimum. Here are a few of them:

1. Run a reverse light cycle. After making sure that the grow room is absolutely free of light leaks during the daylight hours, set the lights to go on at about nine o'clock in the evening (assuming a 12 hour light cycle; the lights going off at 9 a.m.). This schedule permits the use of the cooler night air to help cool the grow room.

2. Try running the air conditioner in the "fan only" cycle during the night. Even without the compressor running or the exchange of any outside air, this technique can be very effective in removing a lot of heat from the air.

3. Increase the frequency of exhaust/injection cycles. For example, a gardener who regularly exhausts for seven minutes once each hour found that his air conditioner came on about twenty minutes after the last exhaust cycle. The air conditioner bounced off and on until the next exhaust cycle. Simply by changing to three shorter exhaust/injection cycles per hour, (and a nighttime "on" cycle), the grower was able to keep the temperature low enough that the air conditioner never came on again. Although the amount of CO_2 used tripled, the savings in electricity was considered to be well worth the extra CO_2 cost and effort.

4. Increase the internal circulation to a virtual blast with strong fans. (Trellis and add supports to the plants if necessary to hold them upright. The additional support may also be needed in the fruiting or flowering phase.) Pay special attention to vertical (floor to ceiling) air circulation.

5. Consider drawing the air from a cooler area. In a two-story house, the first floor remains much cooler during the day than the air in the upstairs. The basement or crawlspace below the house has the coolest air of all. A cool north side of a house

shaded by trees will provide much cooler air than a vent just under the roof line on a side that remains in constant sunshine.

6. One grower buried a network of four inch sewer pipes and drew his incoming air from these pipes. The air was ten degrees cooler than the air entering the intake. (Be certain to screen the intake to prevent against dust and pests. There could also be a mold problem with this arrangement.)

Swamp Coolers

A swamp cooler is a name for an **evaporative cooler**. This is a device that cools the air by circulating water over cedar pads and drawing a high volume of air through the wet pads. The evaporation effect draws a lot of heat from the air. The problem is that some water is put into the air.

Swamp coolers work best in dry climates, where they are most often used in lieu of air conditioning. In dry areas the humidity occasionally stays down in the teens during the hot months. The cool air coming from the swamp cooler can be quite low in humidity.

"Broken" Air Conditioner

An air conditioner that has the compressor unit broken or disconnected can still be of considerable benefit to the grower in a heat-overload situation.

The warm air of the grow room is circulated through the cooling fins of the air conditioner's refrigeration unit, just as in normal operation but without the compressor operating. Although the fins are not as cold as when the energy-sucking compressor is operating, the outside air keeps them much cooler than the grow room air that is circulating through them, and they remove a good bit of heat from the air. By operating the conditioner in the unvented position, no CO_2 is lost to the outside air.

The effectiveness of this method has been demonstrated by a 180 cubic foot growroom running two 1000 watt HPS horizontal lights. (The ballasts were placed in another room, and did not add to the heat in the grow room.) Despite location in an arid part of California, only the air conditioner fan was run. This was during a daylight cycle, in an upstairs apartment, during the summer months.

Remote Conditioning

The "broken" air conditioner concept can work well in a situation where the air conditioner is located some distance from the grow room. In one particular case, the grow chamber was a small cubicle built against an inside upstairs wall in an apartment. The air conditioner was placed in the window in the normal manner, and a wooden enclosure was made for the front of it. Four inch dryer duct hose was used to direct the air to and from the air conditioner to the grow room, which was about 6 feet away. The only power supplied was a small squirrel-cage fan, which provided a positive displacement of air through the cooling fins. The temperature usually dropped about 15 degrees after the air was run through the cooler.

Chapter 7

Humidity Control

Most gardeners are able to win the fight against humidity without resorting to a power-sucking electric dehumidifier. A dehumidifier is something like an air conditioner in operation. Simply plug it in, set the maximum humidity level desired on the humidistat, and the machine will come on and dry the air when the humidity exceeds a set range. Very simple and in-expensive to purchase but expensive to operate if needed full-time. However, they work fairly quickly, and are usually on only a few minutes per hour.

Even so, there are a number of techniques that can be used to lower the humidity before resorting to a dehumidifier.

1. Increase the frequency and/or duration of the ventilation cycles and the size of the exhaust and/or intake fans. Assuming that the humidity is lower outside the room than inside, simply change the air more often, before it has a chance to build up any extra humidity. (Note: there may be times and climatic conditions where the reverse of this practice may lower humidity. When the plants are small - compared to the available cubic feet of space in the grow space - and the outside air is high in humidity, fewer exhaust cycles may lower the overall humidity. This is due to the heating/drying action of the lights.)

2. Increase the internal circulation. Often, in spaces with less than optimum internal air circulation, there will be "pockets"

of high humidity that are caused by an area receiving inadequate circulation. These are usually caused by the plants growing into a canopy, causing two or more microclimates in the grow room. The air above the green canopy is heated and dried by the lights, but the air below the canopy is left relatively cooler and more humid. Gardeners often put their most powerful fans above the canopy, to prevent the heat from the lights from burning the plants. The area below the canopy is often overlooked.

The problem can be remedied by blowing air under the canopy, across the tops of the pots, slabs, or cubes with powerful oscillating fans. The rapid air movement also prevents the formation of mold or rot. The vertical air circulator described elsewhere in this book also helps.

Some gardeners keep internal air circulation at a virtual typhoon-like blast to eliminate temperature and humidity build-up problems. One might assume that since the grow room is a closed environment, increasing the air circulation above moderate levels wouldn't do anything to solve the problems. Wrong! Give it a try before spending big bucks to purchase and operate a dehumidifier.

3. Try taking the air from a different place. Air inside a heated or cooled house usually contains less humidity than the air outside. Changing the intake vent so that air is drawn from the living room instead of the outside can drop the humidity a whole lot. The air may have the added advantage of extra CO_2 from people or pets.

Outside air can also provide different humidity levels. An open sunlight area will usually have lower humidity levels than an area shaded and protected by a lot of trees.

Air taken from the attic is usually lower in humidity than air in the basement. Air taken from the furnace room may be pre-dried of most moisture. There is a trade-off here, of course, since the dry air is probably pretty hot!

Best Locations

The location of the growth chamber in the house or apartment can have a considerable effect on temperature and humidity control. A relatively dry basement is usually the best bet. The basement's wall temperatures can help heat in winter and cool in summer.

A well-insulated house retains the heat of the day after the sun goes down, and remains considerably cooler than the outside air during the day. This can be a big factor in determining whether or not an expensive air conditioner must be installed.

The lack of insulation in a vented attic, or an outside shed, can also be made into a friend. By using a reverse light cycle (lights on during the late night hours and off during the heat of the day), the effects of the temperature fluctuations can be mitigated.

Some research results indicate that plants grown using a cool light cycle and warm dark cycle produce stockier plants. The incoming air flow can be used to condition the room temperature. For example, a second story grow room in a well-insulated two story house can use air from an intake vent that draws air from the living room below, especially if the house is in a hot climate. The air in the living room may be 10 - 15 degrees cooler than the outside air during the day. The downstairs air is also much cooler than the upstairs air.

Chapter 8

Producing CO_2

There are many methods of producing CO_2 for the growth room. Some are quite simple and inexpensive, and some require more complex equipment.

People who have worked with the different methods of CO_2 enhancement say that an automated, fan integrated, cycling injection system is the only way to go. Given proper light and the other factors that are necessary for healthy growth without CO_2, there is no more rewarding investment than installing a good injection system.

Determining the Amount of CO_2 to Release into the Growroom

The first step is to determine the capacity or size of the room in cubic feet. Measure the length $\times$ width $\times$ height of the room. A room that is 10×10 with an 8 foot ceiling is 800 cubic feet.

Determining the amount of CO_2 that must be released to bring the growroom to 1500 ppm is done by multiplying the number of cubic feet in the room by .0015.

$$800 \times .0015 = 1.2$$

1.2 cubic feet of CO_2 gas is required to enrich the air in the room to the desired 1500 ppm of CO_2.

Maxi-CO_2

The 1500 ppm figure is the one given most often in the literature as being ideal. It is by no means absolute, however. One expert puts the ideal at 2000 ppm, and a pair of researchers who obtained excellent results on a Danish ebb-and-flow table used a mere 1300 ppm.

The author of this book feels that 1500 ppm is a good general figure. Perhaps more could be beneficially supplied to some fast-growing species. 2000 or even 2500 ppm may not be too much for some species.

Remember that the plant needs more water and nutrients as the CO_2 levels climb and plant growth spurts. A plant that transpires 1 quart of water daily uses about 2 quarts or more with optimum CO_2 enrichment.

Chapter 9

State-of-the-Art CO_2 Injection and Environmental Controls

Recently several manufacturers have introduced equipment that allows extremely fine control over most of the environmental factors in the high-tech indoor growing environment. These systems that automatically monitor the temperature and humidity, and turn on the exhaust fan or an air-conditioner or dehumidifier any time the temperature or humidity rises above pre-set levels.

After the exhaust cycle is completed, the fan stops and the necessary amount of CO_2 is injected into the air. The injection is facilitated by a small timer that opens the solenoid valve and releases CO_2 for a predetermined number of seconds.

The equipment remains off until one of three things happens:

1. the temperature rises above the predetermined limit,

2. the humidity rises above the predetermined limit or,

3. the amount of time set on the main clock transpires and another cycle is initiated.

Periodic CO_2 Injection

The CO_2 injection system pictured on page 24 contains an integrated fan system. The fan is necessary to remove the stale air

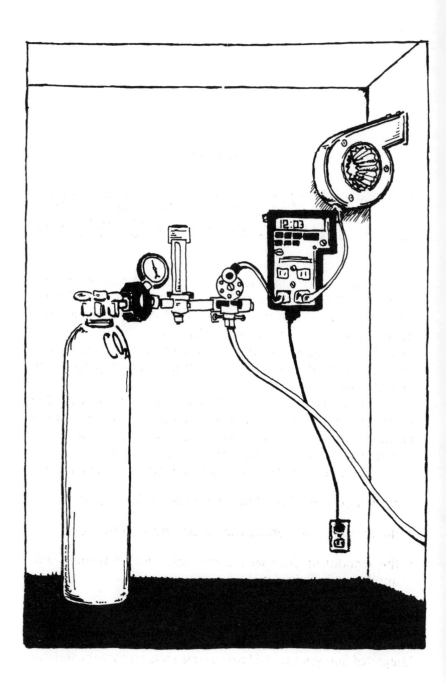

and replace it with clean, fresh air from outside before additional CO_2 is injected into the room. Here is how the system works:

1. The clock timer cycles every hour, causing the mechanism to turn a switch on or off on a minute by minute basis. The clock timer is usually set to turn on the exhaust fan for a certain number of minutes once, twice, or three times an hour.

2. After the fans have exhausted the air in the room and replaced it with fresh air from the outside, CO_2 is injected into the air in adequate amounts to bring the CO_2 levels up to optimum. The CO_2 timer determines the amount of time that the CO_2 release valve remains open, usually measured in seconds.

3. The regulator shows the pressure of gas in the tank and the cubic feet per minute at which the gas is being released when the solenoid valve is opened.

Evacuation/Injection Cycles

There are a number of reasons that growers choose different lengths of time between cycles for the evacuation/injection process. The exhaust fan does a lot more than just change the air to eliminate CO_2 depletion. Artificial lighting often causes a heat build-up. Periodically replacing the hot, stale air with cool, fresh air helps keep the heat within acceptable limits. Also, plants transpire water through their leaves into the air during the growth process. This raises the humidity, which can also make the environment prone to mold and rot, as well as cause loose, stringy plant growth.

Depending on the location, season, placement of the chamber in the house, and other factors, the temperature and humidity changes from day to day. In many cases, simply changing the air and re-injecting CO_2 can cure a problem with temperature or humidity build-up. This is because the heat and moisture-laden air that builds up in the room is replaced with cool, fresh, drier air from the outside.

Seasonal changes in the weather often result in alterations to the time between evacuation/injection cycles. For example, as the temperature heats up in the summer, more frequent cycles are necessary because the air being drawn into the chamber is considerably warmer to begin with, and therefore rises more quickly to the point where the temperature is unduly high. In some locales, more cycles may be warranted in the winter rainy season, because the air being drawn into the room contains more moisture.

Tubing and CO_2 Dispersion

CO_2 must be introduced into the grow room in the proper manner for it to do its job correctly. Some equipment manufacturers recommend a perforated tube strung around the ceiling with small holes to let the cool CO_2 fall down over the plants. This is a must in a grow room with inadequate internal circulation, but the CO_2 probably won't do much in these circumstances. It quickly falls to the floor and escapes through cracks in the baseboards in a room with improper internal circulation.

Large, heavy duty, oscillating fans are the solution. You just can't get too much air blowing around in the growth chamber, both above and below the green canopy. (See drawing on page 28.)

CO_2 Tanks

A CO_2 tank can be a monster. Even the little ones can be little monsters! Why? Because they weigh far more than most people estimate . . . especially half way up a few flights of stairs.

The smaller tanks are referred to as twenty pound CO_2 cylinders. That is because they hold 20 pounds of CO_2 gas. But don't let the nomenclature fool you. A twenty pound steel tank weighs about 50 pounds when full. A full fifty pound tank weighs about 170 pounds.

Tanks are available for sale or rental at welding supply companies. This is where a tank is re-filled. (Usually the empty tank is swapped for a full one.)

CO$_2$ tanks are regularly used by welders, bars, and people with home beer tappers.

Always protect the valve from being knocked off or damaged in an industrial accident. Always chain the tank to the wall in an upright position to prevent accidental tip-over.

Regulator Freeze - Up

Gas is extremely cold when it escapes from the tank. A quick blast can do damage to skin tissue or eyes. Be careful!

CO$_2$ can also freeze and ruin a regulator. In haste to supply CO$_2$ to the waiting plants, many growers crank the regulator up to a flow-rate that can cause cause regulator freeze-up. This can occur at anything above 20 CFH (**cubic feet per hour**). Special heated regulators are available for those with a large area, or a shortage of patience.

Determining CO$_2$ Release Time

At 20 cfh, each minute of CO$_2$ release yields one-third of a cubic foot of CO$_2$ released. A 10 × 10 × 8 foot room would require a little over 3 minutes of CO$_2$ release.

Advantages of Injection

1. Periodic injection of CO$_2$ is very clean.

2. Precise control of CO$_2$ levels is easy.

3. Injection does not add to temperature or humidity.

4. When injected into a powerful fan or through a perforated tube suspended from the ceiling, the CO$_2$ is easily dispersed throughout entire growing area.

5. There is no danger from flame, heat or flammable gas.

Disadvantages of Injection

1. An injection system requires handling of heavy tanks which must be taken in and out of growing area on a regular basis for refilling.

2. The cost is high for the initial equipment, then very low for the CO$_2$ itself (compared to other methods).

3. A very slight danger is present from valve damage causing the tank to become an uncontrolled projectile powered by gas escaping at up 1000 pounds per square inch of pressure.

4. Another slight danger (although probably more likely to happen than the previous scenario) is the displacement of air that can happen in the event of quick release of all the CO$_2$ in a tank into a closed area. Both plant and human can perish in this event. Not because CO$_2$ is a poisonous gas, but because the CO$_2$ can displace all the oxygen in the area, causing asphyxiation, or death from lack of oxygen.

The author of this book was nearly asphyxiated while running a machine that was activated by CO$_2$ release, causing a slow but steady build-up of CO$_2$ in the room, gradually displacing all the oxygen.

Asphyxiation symptoms come on slowly. They begin with a sleepy and lethargic feeling, and can be followed by a desire to lay down for a nap. There are no "danger sign" feelings in the lungs. If you feel this way when in your growing chamber, get out quickly! Check your equipment for signs of malfunction later.

Chapter 10

CO_2 Combustion Generators

The CO_2 generator has long been a fixture of commercial greenhouse growers. Unlike the injection system, the generator works by constantly creating CO_2, instead of releasing enough to treat an entire room at one time.

The generator is often used in greenhouses because the structures are drafty and the CO_2 enhancement would be soon lost if the release was intermittent. The process used by commercial CO_2 generators is quite simple. A clean burning gas such as propane or natural gas is burned through a burner like is found in a stove or furnace. Each pound of gas burned yields about 3 pounds of CO_2, or about 25 cubic feet.

The generation principal works on all levels. Large commercial generators are used in greenhouses and large area growth chambers. A simple and small alcohol lamp can be used in a closet growth chamber to provide CO_2 enhancement, although I cannot recommend a flame in a room with combustible materials.

Advantages of Generation

1. Equipment can purchased for all size systems.

2. If the house containing the grow chamber is plumbed with natural gas, there is no need to haul around large tanks.

3. An alcohol lamp type generator uses only a gallon or so of alcohol each week (much less for the small closet type operation). This is easily transported into areas where propane or CO_2 tanks may present a problem. Alcohol fuel can usually be purchased at any hardware store.

Disadvantages of Generation

1. Flames always contain an inherent danger of catastrophic fire.

2. Generation of CO_2 by burning puts heat and water vapor into the air. The heat may be unwanted, the water vapor can always present a problem.

3. It is not recommended, and is usually illegal with good reason, to keep a pressurized tank of propane in a closed area.

4. Incorrectly plumbed gas fittings may leak creating a fire/explosion/asphyxiation hazard.

5. A knocked over lantern or alcohol lamp can instantly become a roaring inferno. Since the alcohol flames burn with an almost totally clear flame, the fire can get a good start before it's noticed, even if the grower is in the room!

6. A flame can use up all the oxygen in the air, resulting in asphyxiation in a tightly closed area.

Chapter 11

Producing CO_2 through Fermentation

Fermentation is the process by which beer, wine, whiskey, and other alcoholic beverages are produced. Fruit, sugar, or starch bearing materials are put into solution with water and yeast are added. Yeast are tiny organisms that eat the sugar and produce CO_2 and alcohol as bodily wastes. The yeast reproduce very rapidly and more and more yeast eat the sugar and produce alcohol and CO_2. They soon raise the alcohol level in their environment above 10%, which causes the yeast to stop metabolizing.

Indoor hobbyists have used the fermentation method for a few years now, and it is recognized as a reliable and inexpensive way to manufacture CO_2.

Homebrew

Some hobbyists use the fermentation system because they like the second hobby - home beer and wine making! A few five gallon jugs of quality homebrew, or a few wooden casks of wine, can greatly enhance the output of a growing chamber. With inexpensive and accurate CO_2 test kits now available, it is possible for a hobbyist to determine the amount of brew that must be working to keep his grow room at the desired ppm of CO_2.

Producing CO_2 through Fermentation

There are many books on home beer and wine making, and almost every city usually has a store that sells beer and wine making supplies. If the supplies are not available in your area, check the Yellow Pages or mail order companies.

Simple Small Scale Fermentation

If the fermentation method meets your needs as a system of CO_2 enhancement, but you have no desire to produce drinking alcohol, the process is very simple. Sugar, water, and yeast from the grocery store are used to make a simple brew that produces CO_2 at a fairly regular rate for about 3 to 4 days. At this time the spent solution is dumped and a new brew started.

Gallon Jug CO_2 Fermentation

1. Make a starter mixture of a half cup of sugar and a pinch of yeast (distiller's yeast is best) in 12 ounces of water. Set this in a warm place until it starts bubbling.

2. Make a mixture of two pounds of sugar in six quarts of water in a three or four gallon plastic jug.

3. Poke a small hole in the top of the cap and put the bubbling froth in the grow room. Although the simple hole poked in the top of a milk jug cap works fine most of the time, many growers follow the advice of home beer brewers and attach a fermentation lock to the top of the mixture. This equipment serves two purposes. It bubbles the CO_2 through water so that the rate of production is easily observed and calculated, and it prevents contaminants from entering the fermentation mixture.

4. When the bubbling slows down after about three days, add a bit of the old mixture to another fresh batch of sugar water, and discard the old mixture. The new one should start working in a few hours. Remember to keep the temperature below 95 degrees and above 80 degrees. (See drawing on page 34.)

Larger Scale, Continuous Batch Fermentation

Using approximately the same ratios of sugar and water as described above, a large scale fermentation can be kept going for up to two months. Start with a large tub, tank, or trash can. Add a gallon of sugar water every day or two and see how high it keeps the CO_2 levels in the grow room. Be sure to leave lots of room for additional liquid as the tank fills. Remember that cleanliness, and a good air lock, are the keys to a long-lasting fermentation. (See drawing on page 36.)

CO_2 from sugar is an expensive method of production. If the brew is used for consumption, or the alcohol is to be distilled for fuel, it makes sense economically.

Advantages of Fermentation

1. The system can be set up very inexpensively.

2. The process uses common materials.

3. Utilization of fermentation to make CO_2 for a growth chamber can provide home brewed beer, wine or fuel as a by-product of the process.

4. The process uses no heat, flame, gas, flammable liquid, or electricity.

Disadvantages of Fermentation

1. The process can get messy.

2. The fermentation process can present an odor problem.

3. Continuous generation is not as efficient as periodic injection of an amount sufficient to treat the entire room in one rapid release.

4. It is difficult to achieve fairly uniform CO_2 levels from one day to the next. This is because there is fluctuation in the amount of CO_2 generated at different phases of the fermentation, and there are a myriad of factors which can effect each fermentation, causing different levels of CO_2 to be produced.

Floral Beer

Floral Beer is a phenomenon with a rather limited but enthusiastic following among the scientific/horticultural community around California's Bay Area and Silicon Valley.

It is made by soaking aromatic plants in homemade beer while the beer is brewing. The alcohol in the beer removes the aromatic essences of the flowers or leaves being soaked, and imparts unusual qualities to the beer.

In some recipes the water-soluble chlorophyll and pigments of the flowers or leaves being soaked are removed prior to the beer-making process.

The plant material is first soaked for about 8 hours in cold water, with a minimum of agitation. It is then rinsed, the flowers are dried and then added to the batch of beer in a large cheesecloth sack. The soaking and rinse water are discarded. The sack is allowed to remain in the brew during the entire process. It is removed prior to bottling.

Chapter 12

Dry Ice

Dry ice is simply frozen CO_2. It is inexpensive and readily available. Look under "dry ice" in the Yellow Pages. Unlike water, CO_2 has no liquid stage at atmospheric pressures. It transforms directly from solid to gas as it thaws.

A pound of dry ice equals a pound of CO_2. A pound of CO_2 equals 8.7 cubic feet. By timing the period required for a chunk of a certain size to melt, a fairly good estimate can be made of the amount of CO_2 put into the atmosphere during that time period.

Some practitioners utilize a block of dry ice put into an insulating device such as a foam ice cooler with holes cut into the top and sides. The size and number of holes allow control of the rate at which the block melts and releases CO_2. (See drawing on page 38.)

Advantages of Dry Ice

1. Dry ice is inexpensive and easily obtained.

2. Dry ice is non-toxic, but the extreme cold can damage tissue. Wear insulated gloves when moving unwrapped chunks. (Pants of some sort are also a good idea around large exposed chunks of dry ice.)

3. Dry ice requires no flame, electricity, or moving parts to use.

4. Dry ice is compact and more easily moved than tanks of CO_2 gas.

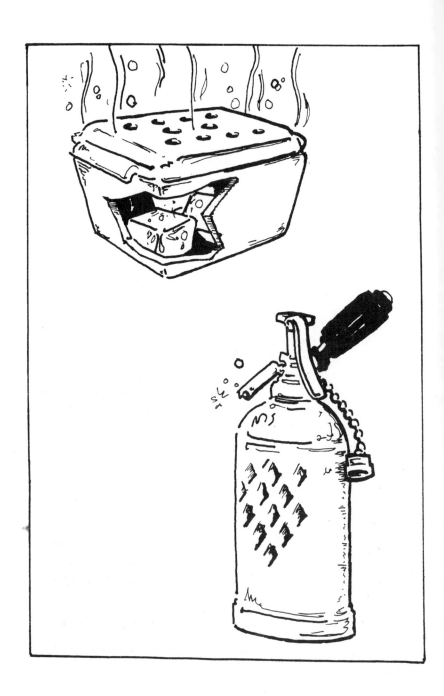

5. Dry ice does not put any heat or water into the atmosphere. The frozen CO_2 actually helps to control heat due to the fact that of dry ice remains frozen below 100 degrees below zero!

Disadvantages of Dry Ice

1. The continuous generation of CO_2 gas limits the use of exhaust fan cycles.

2. There is a period of less than optimum CO_2 levels while the room is slowly filling.

3. While the melting rate can be slowed by keeping dry ice in a food freezer, it can not be stopped. It is difficult to store dry ice at home.

Chapter 13

Seltzer Water

Some growers spray their plants with seltzer water. This drink is composed of water and CO_2 and the CO_2 is released as the water evaporates. This practice could get expensive with a large room full of plants, especially considering that, in order to produce measurable results, the CO_2 should be replenished every hour or so. (This, of course, could lead to mold and rot, especially if the grower is producing flowering plants that are approaching maturity.)

If this method really appeals to you, consider an old-time seltzer bottle. Water is put into a reinforced bottle equipped with a holder for a small CO_2 "charger" of the type used in a BB gun. The released gas carbonates the water (adds CO_2) and also provides pressure to squirt out the liquid when the valve is opened. A seltzer fanatic could pre-mix fertilizer, hormones, or cloning solution in the bottle.

A variation of this method is practiced by some commercial growers, who report higher yields. CO_2 is bubbled through the nutrient solution tank prior to a watering cycle.

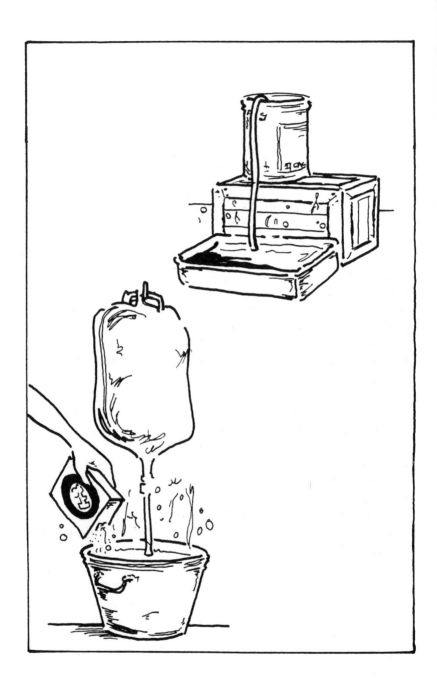

Chapter 14

The Soda/Acid Generation Method

Generation of CO_2 in the grow room by dripping vinegar (acetic acid) into a bed of baking soda is a recent development in the world of indoor gardens. (See drawing on page 42.) This method is best suited for a small closet type operation. There is no temperature rise, no water vapor is created, and there is no risk of fire. Although the equipment to generate CO_2 chemically is inexpensive, the cost of the vinegar and baking soda makes this an expensive method.

Compared to timed cycles of exhaust followed by injection, the continuous drip soda/acid method lags far behind injection in its capacity to produce and maintain the optimum levels of CO_2 for best growth. This is due to its process of continuous but slow release of CO_2.

Assuming that we are working with a grow area with a timed exhaust cycle, the gas generated from the continuous drip soda/acid method would start out at just above the 300 ppm available in the air drawn into the growth chamber from outside. As the vinegar drips into the soda, CO_2 is continuously formed and the CO_2 level in the room rises. It usually takes a considerable portion of the cycle for the CO_2 to build to the point where it does much good. If the CO_2 is generated too rapidly, it can reach levels where it is detrimental and even toxic to the plants.

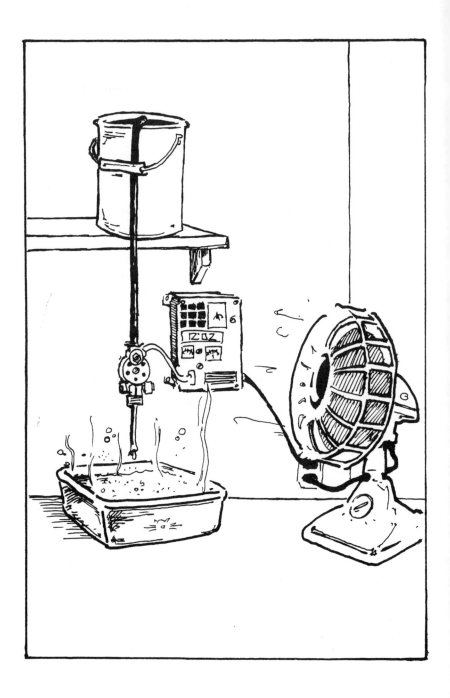

Cyclic Vinegar Dump Device

The accompanying illustration shows a design for a CO_2 device that periodically drops an easily regulated amount of vinegar into a bed of soda. The solenoid operated dump valve dispenses the vinegar into the soda after completion of the periodic exhaust cycle. The CO_2 generation is safe, rapid, and similar in many aspects to release of CO_2 from a timed injection system.

This system is unavailable commercially, and I have not tried the design, but construction and operation should be straightforward.

It is important to find a timer that permits settings of at least one opening per hour, and will dispense the vinegar without any pressure.

There are a lot of complex formulas that can be used to determine how much of what to add how often. The best bet is to make a rough guess, and then set the system up in the manner in which it will be operated. Be prepared to take a number of tests with the glass tube/syringe CO_2 tester. Take the test after the first vinegar dump, and then adjust the burette or IV bottle by increasing or decreasing the rate at which it fills to a point where it will contain more or less vinegar when the next exhaust/vinegar dump cycle occurs.

The variables in this piece of equipment (dump cycle and fill rate) are easily controlled. The settings that produce 1500 ppm one time should do the job pretty much the same way every time.

Chapter 15

Weird & Exotic Methods of CO₂ Manufacture and Application

Cows in the Growroom?

There has been mention in popular literature of different animals being allowed to enter the growing chamber, to provide CO_2 via the air they exhale. In the most common situation, an indoor growing room or chamber in a house or apartment, the only animal that should be allowed in is the human animal.

Cats, dogs, raccoons, gerbils, boa constrictors, or whatever you might like to let slither around the home can bring in all sorts of undesirable pests.

It is possible to draw the incoming air from a remote room or area. It is also possible to filter the incoming air to remove bugs, dust, and other airborne particulates. Although the opportunity probably won't present itself very often, there may be situations where the incoming air can be taken from a room that is regularly kept full of animals or humans. Simply test the air with a CO_2 tester. If the levels are noticeably above those in the outside air, consider taking air from this area.

Bovine Flatulence

Growing areas above the barn in the hayloft are probably relatively common in agricultural communities. Cattle are one of the most prodigious producers of CO_2 in the world. The cud-chewing process teams up with a multiple stomach system and . . . presto! A veritable bovine CO_2 factory. Scientists have listed cud-chewing and bovine flatulence as major contributing factors to the greenhouse effect. A growth chamber in a barn above a large amount of cattle may have CO_2 exceeding the desired levels.

Composted CO_2

A compost heap is a pile of decaying matter such as leaves, twigs, plant clippings, etc. Large amounts of CO_2 are released during the process through fermentation. A good compost turns 100 pounds (wet weight) of organic material such as leaves or plant trimmings into 50 pounds or more of CO_2. The fermentation process takes about a month, and releases CO_2 in fairly regular daily amounts once the digesting action begins.

Starting a compost in a grow room would be a very messy and unsanitary proposition, but there are probably several "country" applications wherein a compost system could supply clean and adequate CO_2 to a greenhouse or larger growing operation.

The compost heap could be started in a cement, brick or adobe "oven" with a length of stove pipe drawing the CO_2 into the greenhouse or growth area. An air filtration system would be necessary in this system. Large spun glass furnace filters should work well.

Warning

Fermentation via composting can also produce quantities of methane, a poisonous and explosive gas. It is strongly recommended that the practitioner take steps to prevent all situations that could be hazardous when using a composting situation to produce CO$_2$. It's highly unlikely, but both the composting chamber and the greenhouse could become explosive. Know what you are doing via lots of additional study before you try this one.

Human CO$_2$

The hobbyist himself can be a supplier of CO$_2$. Simply spending time in the growing area adds to the CO$_2$ level. Not enough to prevent depletion in a closed room, or enough to enhance the atmosphere to anywhere near the 1500 ppm level, but enough that plant growth increases.

Chapter 16

Exhaust and Odor Control

Odor control can be a big problem, especially in an apartment building, or other close-quarters living. Almost everybody loves the smell of roses, but gardens may be too odoriferous in enclosed areas, such as apartments. If you are using the fermentation method of CO_2 enrichment, the pungent odor of your beer or sugar-water brew may make enemies of your nearest neighbors. It is always best to try to keep the smells to a minimum.

Skunk Buster

There are a number of ways to handle odors. The best by far is a heavy duty charcoal and electrostatic air filtration device. The most popular brand is called a Skunk Buster. The device is simply plugged into an electric outlet in the room containing the plants, and the smell is quickly removed from the air. Unless the room is vented directly into someone's smell zone, the odor problem is eliminated.

Negative Ion Generators

After living with these things for many years, the author has come to appreciate ionizers as being wonders of technology.

Used in the grow room, ionizers take a lot of the smell out of the air. By no means all of it, and by no means as much as a Skunk Buster. As a side benefit, both research and the author's hands-on experience confirm that the plants grow obviously better and faster in the presence of the generator. It is difficult to measure added vigor, even in a well designed and executed scientific experiment, but the practical results seem to verify the effect.

Where To Exhaust

Air can usually be exhausted out a window, bathroom vent, or into the attic. It is always better to take the air up through a vent or chimney through the roof.

Odor Control Inside the House

A situation that many growers have to face is the slight odor of the growing plants or fermentation permeating throughout the house. No odor outside, but let someone take one step inside the house or apartment, and they immediately notice the unusual smells.

An ionizer anywhere outside the grow room usually gets rid of migrating odors very effectively. An ionizer or Skunk Buster inside the grow room will usually get rid of the odors before they get out to become a problem.

A "whole house" fan that continuously empties the house air into the attic or out a window can change the air in the house rapidly enough that lingering odors are soon removed.

CO_2 and the Environment

CO_2 sold in tanks or dry ice form is usually **captured** as a by-product from another industrial process. If it were not collected, it would be released into the atmosphere. We state this because many growers are very environmentally consciousness and the idea of contributing to the so-called greenhouse effect no doubt causes mental grief to these growers.

CO_2 produced through fermentation, soda/acid, or composting is just that - produced CO_2. Growers using these methods are actually contributing to the CO_2 in the atmosphere.